Make ART Make Mistakes

A Creativity Sketchbook

chronicle books·san francisco

MoMA
modern
kids

Don't worry
Making things
mistakes,

about mistakes.
out of
that's creativity.

PETER MAX

A line is a dot that went for a walk. PAUL KLEE

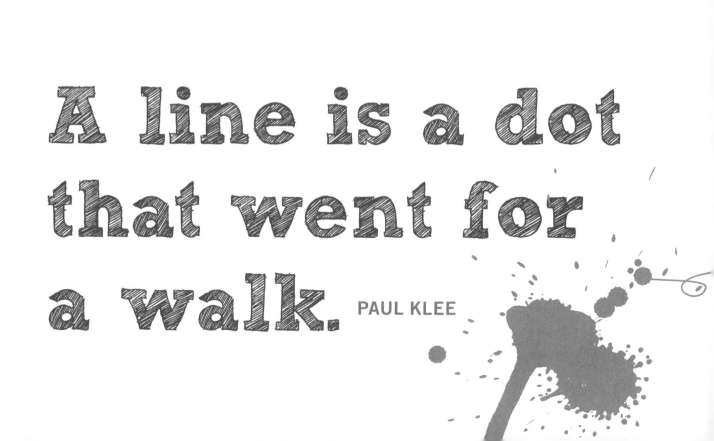

DRAW MANY DIFFERENT
TYPES OF LINES.

What would a lazy line look like?

How about an angry line?

An excited line?

A silly line?

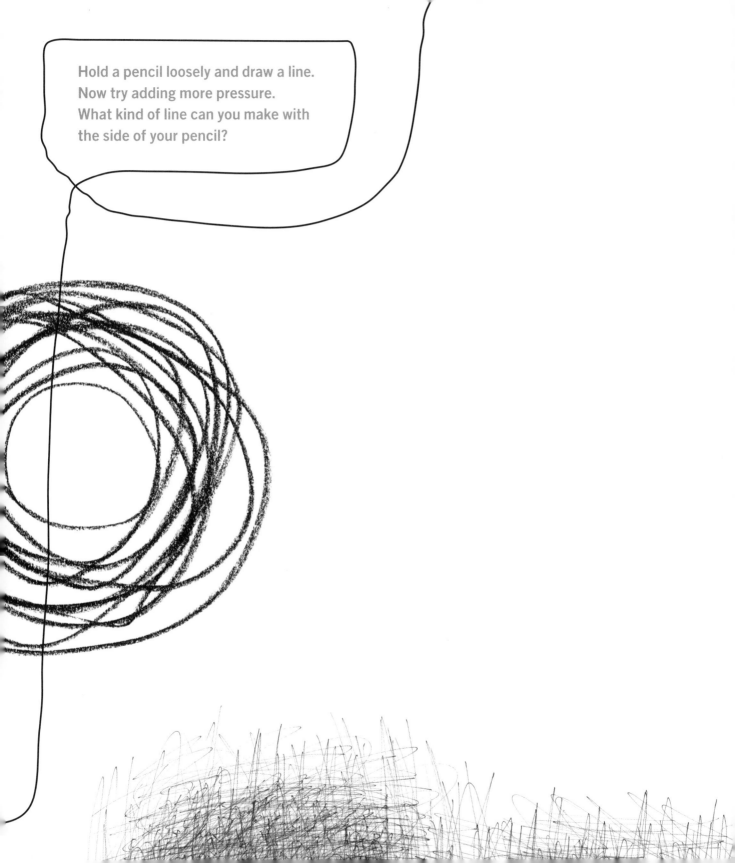

Hold a pencil loosely and draw a line.
Now try adding more pressure.
What kind of line can you make with
the side of your pencil?

Shade this page using the side of a pencil. Use an eraser to create lines through the shading.

Draw a portrait of a person using only 10 lines.

Now try to draw a portrait using only 5 lines.

Can you draw a portrait using only 3 lines?

Create five marks on the page.
How can you connect them to create a face or a figure?

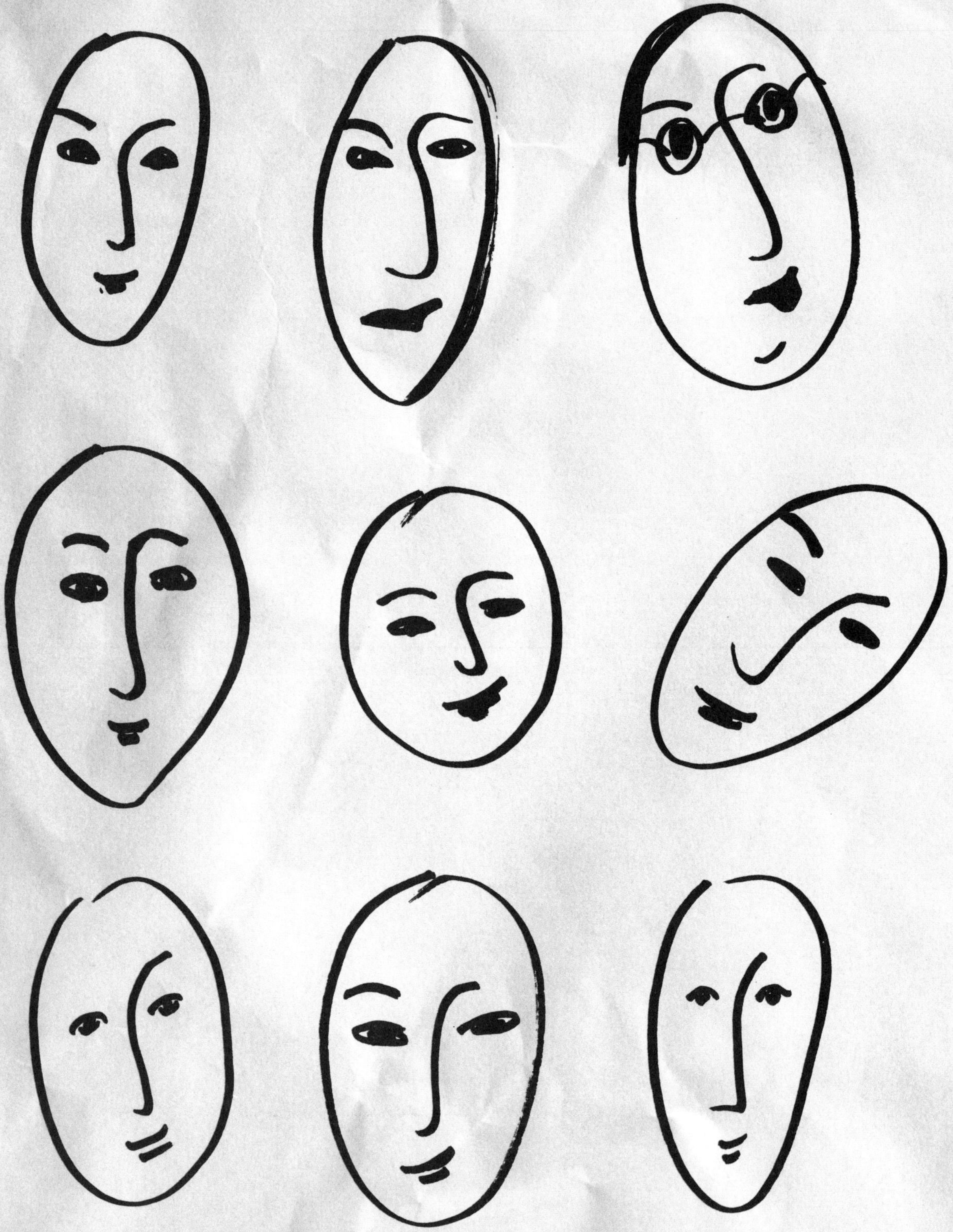

Draw a portrait of a person without using any straight lines.

Fill this page with doodles of your own.

Have no fear of perfection— you'll never reach it. SALVADOR DALI

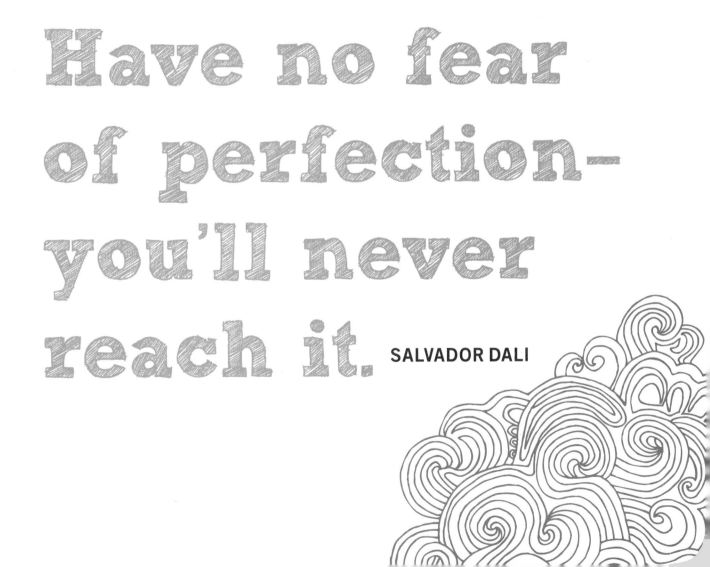

Draw a tall building, using the lines in the graph paper to create windows and doors.

Using one line, create the outline of the buildings, houses, or trees that you see along the horizon.

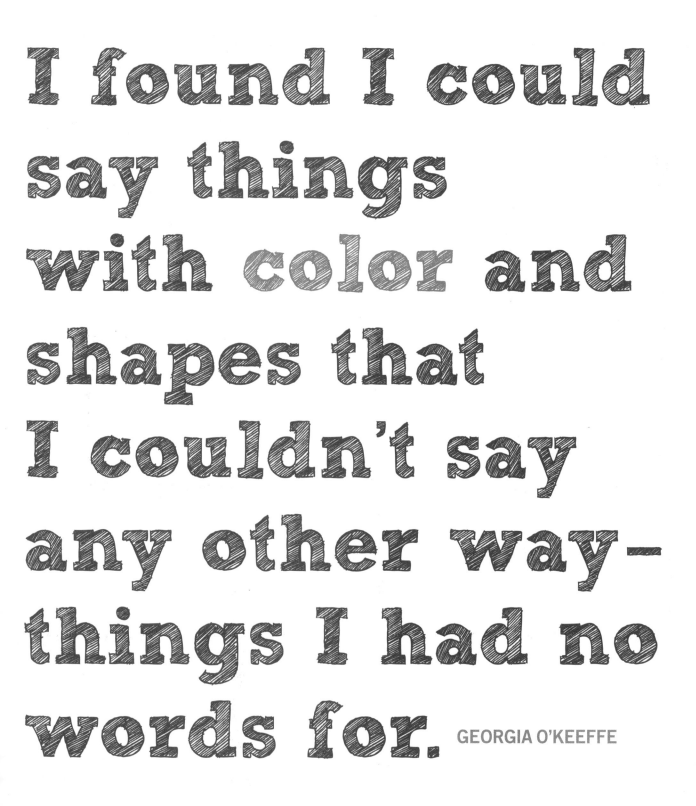

I found I could say things with color and shapes that I couldn't say any other way— things I had no words for. GEORGIA O'KEEFFE

Create a grid and fill in each square with a color.
Will you create a pattern?

Make a self-portrait using your favorite colors.

How might you show blue and red dancing?

Draw a fight between yellow and purple.

What would three colors at play look like?

Pick a color. What ten words come to mind as you look at the color?
Write them down and arrange the words to create a color poem.

Now, look around you for that color. Record what you see using drawings or words.

CREATE A COLOR WHEEL.

Color the shades in between the primary colors.

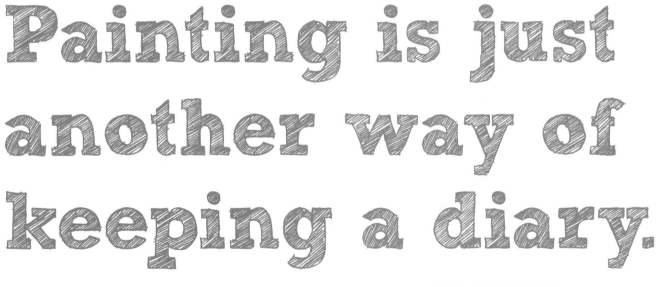

Painting is just another way of keeping a diary.

PABLO PICASSO

If your mood today was a color, which color would it be? Fill the page with that color.

Use the squares below to record the color of the sky at three different times of day.

DATE/TIME: DATE/TIME: DATE/TIME:

Can you create a pattern out of these three colors?

LOOK OUT YOUR WINDOW.
WHAT DO YOU SEE?

Try drawing the view using only five colors.

Now draw the same view using only three of the colors you chose.

Can you draw it using only two colors?

Look at the colors people around you are wearing.
Using rectangles of color in place of the people, create a color composition.
Draw small rectangles for people that are far away and bigger rectangles
for those people closest to you.

DRAW A SHAPE, THEN COLOR

OUTSIDE OF THE LINES!

I search for
realness, the
real feeling
of a subject,
all the texture
around it...

ANDREW WYETH

Think of a texture. How might you show that texture in a drawing?

What does smooth look like?

What does bumpy look like?

How can you show fuzzy?

What was the last fruit or vegetable that you ate? Can you draw its texture?

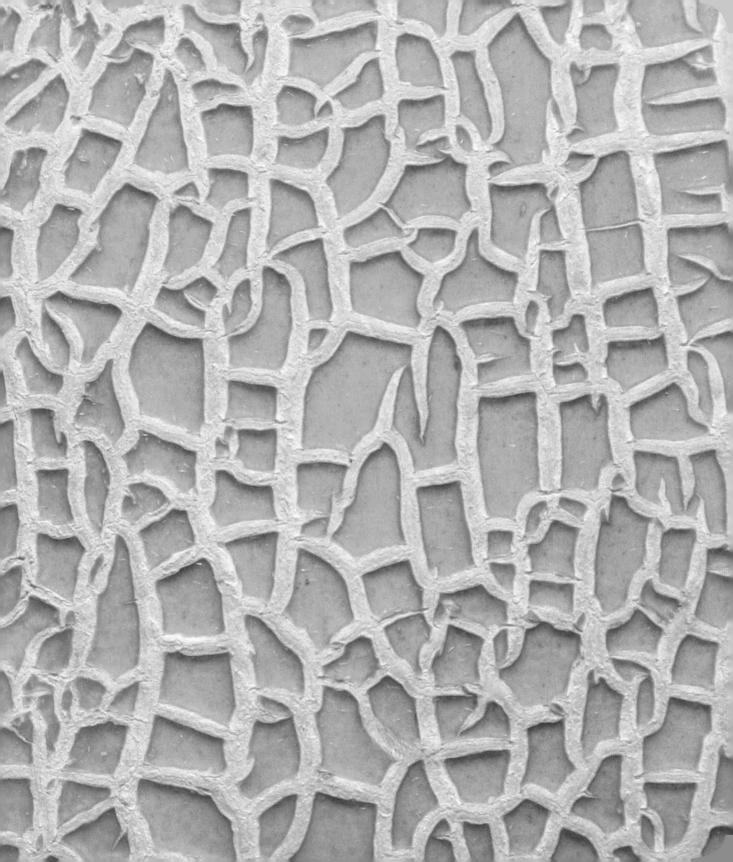

Fill the page with rubbings of textures.you come across.
If you want, record what they are and where you found them.

Use your shoe to make a print on the page. What do you notice about the texture? Experiment with stamping your shoe in different directions. What else might you use as a stamp?

Look closely at the many textures of a wood floor. Try to re-create the grain.

Make a list of words that describe the surface of water in motion.
Can you use them to write a poem about water?

I build a painting by putting little marks together—some look like hot dogs, others like doughnuts.

CHUCK CLOSE

CREATE A PATTERN THAT USES LINES.

Try one of the following:

Use alternating types of lines (straight, spiraled, zig-zag).

Use only one type of line (for example, make a row of diagonals).

Create a pattern using only circles.
Try making them all the same size.
Then try making them different sizes.

Make a pattern using only diamonds.
Change the pattern by turning the diamond in different directions.

* % * % * % * % * % *

Think of a familiar symbol and use it to make a pattern.

※ * % * % * % * % *

Create a pattern using the first letter of your name and flipping the letter in different directions.

Create a pattern using two of the colors you are wearing.

Then create the same pattern using two different colors.

Create a pattern using a shape you find in nature, such as a cloud.

Create a pattern using shapes from your imagination.

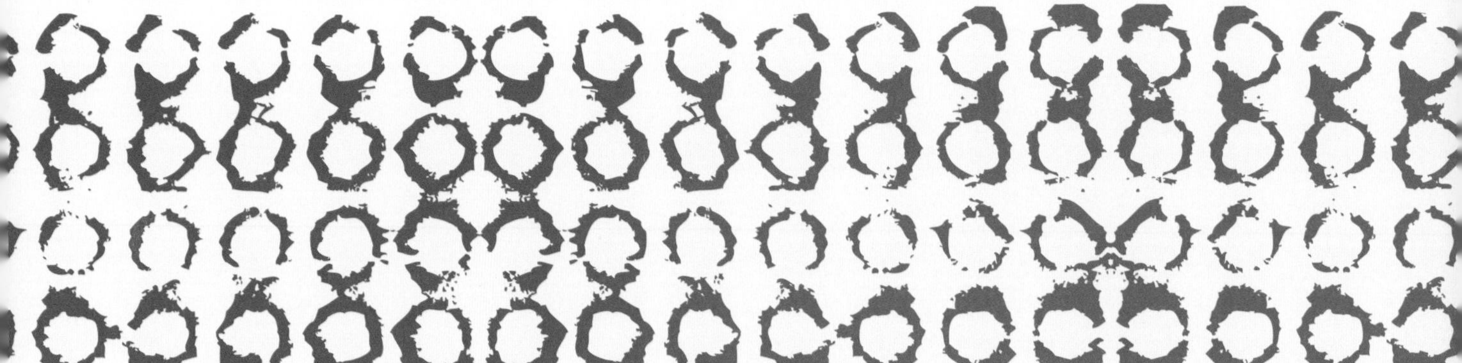

I will make

mistakes, but...

I will not make any more boring art.
I will not make any more boring art.
I will not make any more boring art.
I will not make any more boring art.
I will not make any more boring art.
I will not make any more boring art.
I will not make any more boring art.
I will not make any more boring art.
I will not make any more boring art.
I will not make any more boring art.
I will not make any more boring art.
I will not make any more boring art.
I will not make any more boring art.
I will not make any more boring art.
I will not make any more boring art.
I will not make any more boring art.
I will not make any more boring art.
I will not make any more boring art.
I will not make any more boring art.
I will not make any more boring art.
I will not make any more boring art.
I will not make any more boring art.
I will not make any more boring art.
I will not make any more boring art.
I will not make any more boring art.
I will not make any more boring art.

I will not make any more boring art.
I will not make any more boring art.
I will not make any more boring art.
I will not make any more boring art.
I will not make any more boring art.
I will not make any more boring art.
I will not make any more boring art.
I will not make any more boring art.
I will not make any more boring art.
I will not make any more boring art.
I will not make any more boring art.
I will not make any more boring art.
I will not make any more boring art.
I will not make any more boring art.
I will not make any more boring art.
I will not make any more boring art.
I will not make any more boring art.
I will not make any more boring art.
I will not make any more boring art.
I will not make any more boring art.
I will not make any more boring art.
I will not make any more boring art.
I will not make any more boring art.
I will not make any more boring art.
I will not make any more boring art.
I will not make any more boring art.
I will not make any more boring art.
I will not make any more boring art.

IMAGES PAGES 6–7, 12–13, 22–23, 32–33, 34, 36, 42, 51, 56, 57, 62, 65, 66–67, 68–69, 74–75, 76–77, 80, 88–89, 90, 93, 98–99, 107, 108 © istockphoto.com. Page 39 © Illustration Works, Inc.

All other images © Chronicle Books, LLC.

I Will Not Make Any More Boring Art
John Baldessari (American, born 1931)

1971. Lithograph, composition: 22 3/8 x 29 9/16" (56.8 x 75.1 cm); sheet: 22 7/16 x 30 1/16" (57 x 76.4 cm). Publisher: The Nova Scotia College of Art and Design, Halifax. Printer: Nova Scotia College of Art and Design Lithography Workshop, Halifax. Edition: 50. John B. Turner Fund. © 2010 John Baldessari.

Concept developed by Chronicle Books for MoMA.

Copyright © 2010 The Museum of Modern Art, New York, NY 10019.

The Museum of Modern Art, MoMA, and the MoMA logo are registered trademarks and/or trademarks of The Museum of Modern Art in the United States and certain other countries.

The Museum of Modern Art

ISBN 978-0-8118-7076-4

Manufactured by Leo Paper Products, Heshan, China, in January 2015.

10 9 8 7 6

This product conforms to CPSIA 2008 and ASTM F963 safety standards.

Chronicle Books LLC
680 Second Street
San Francisco, California 94107
www.chroniclekids.com